Empress Wu Zetian

CHERRY LAKE PRESS

Published in the United States of America by Cherry Lake Publishing Group
Ann Arbor, Michigan
www.cherrylakepublishing.com

Reading Adviser: Beth Walker Gambro, MS, Ed., Reading Consultant, Yorkville, IL
Book Design: Jennifer Wahi
Illustrator: Jeff Bane

Photo Credits: © Liu zishan/Shutterstock, 5; 未知, Public domain, via Wikimedia Commons, 7; © Shan_shan/Shutterstock, 9; © Zhang zhicheng, CC BY-SA 3.0 via Wikimedia Commons, 11 and 22; © beibaoke/Shutterstock, 13 and 23; © kentoh/Shutterstock, 15; © HelloRF Zcool/Shutterstock, 17; © otnaydur/Shutterstock, 19; Unknown author, Public domain, via Wikimedia Commons, 21

Cherry Lake Press is an imprint of Cherry Lake Publishing Group

Library of Congress Cataloging-in-Publication Data

Names: Loh-Hagan, Virginia, author. | Bane, Jeff, 1957- illustrator.
Title: Empress Wu Zetian / written by Virginia Loh-Hagan ; [illustrated by Jeff Bane]
Description: Ann Arbor, Michigan : Cherry Lake Publishing, [2024] | Series: My itty-bitty bio | Audience: Grades K-1 | Summary: "Empress Wu Zetian is still known today as one of the greatest emperors in the history of China. This biography for early readers examines her life in a simple, age-appropriate way that helps young readers develop word recognition and reading skills. This title helps all readers learn about a historical female leader who made a difference in our world. The My Itty-Bitty Bio series celebrates diversity and inclusion, values that readers of all ages can aspire to"-- Provided by publisher.
Identifiers: LCCN 2023035022 | ISBN 9781668937747 (hardcover) | ISBN 9781668938782 (paperback) | ISBN 9781668940129 (ebook) | ISBN 9781668941478 (pdf)
Subjects: LCSH: Wu hou, Empress of China, 624-705--Juvenile literature. | Empresses--China--Biography--Juvenile literature. | China--History--Tang dynasty, 618-907--Juvenile literature.
Classification: LCC DS749.42.W8 L64 2023 | DDC 951/.017092 [B]--dc23/eng/20230801
LC record available at https://lccn.loc.gov/2023035022

Printed in the United States of America

table of contents

My Story 4

Timeline 22

Glossary 24

Index 24

About the author: When not writing, Dr. Virginia Loh-Hagan serves as the Director of the Asian Pacific Islander Desi American (APIDA) Center at San Diego State University. She is also the Co-Executive Director of The Asian American Education Project. She lives in San Diego with her very tall husband and very naughty dogs.

About the illustrator: Jeff Bane and his two business partners own a studio along the American River in Folsom, California, home of the 1849 Gold Rush. When Jeff's not sketching or illustrating for clients, he's either swimming or kayaking in the river to relax.

I was born in 624. I lived in China.

Have you been to China?

I was a girl. I was not meant to rule. I was meant to serve.

I was smart. I loved to read.
I read about many things.

What do you like to read about?

I worked at the royal **court**. I was 14 years old. I charmed everyone.

I married the emperor. I ruled China. I had big ideas.

I opened trade. I **expanded** the Chinese **empire**. I made China rich. I brought peace.

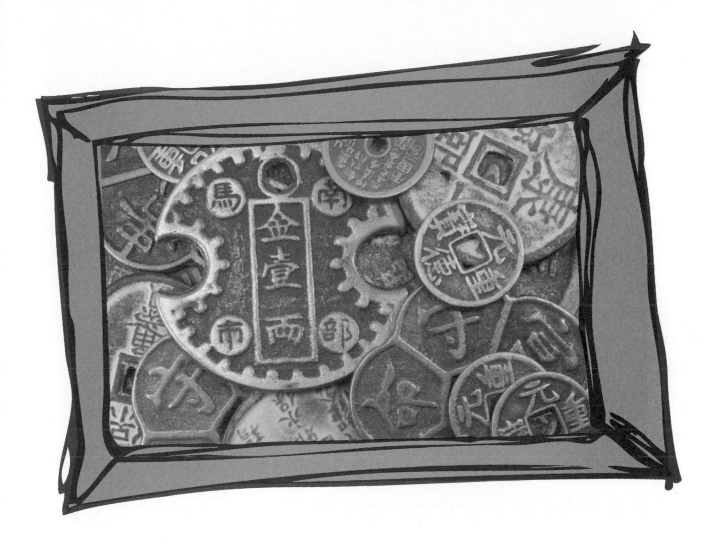

I gave people more freedoms.
I wanted them to learn. I wanted
them to have jobs.

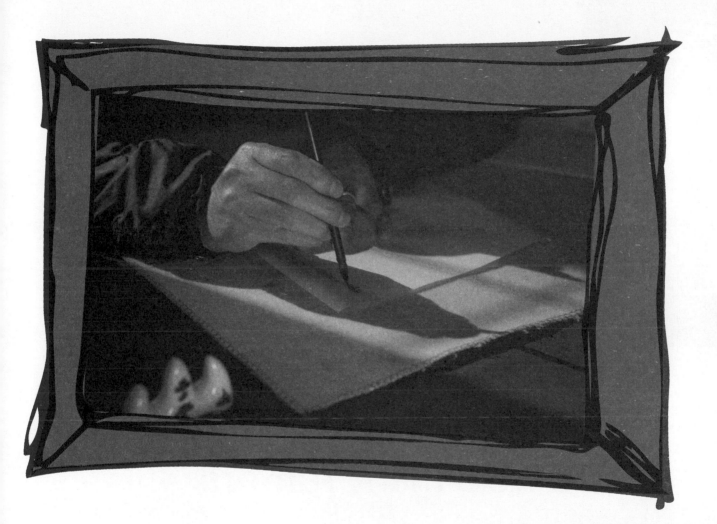

Not everyone liked me.
They didn't like women rulers.
There were many **rumors**
about me.

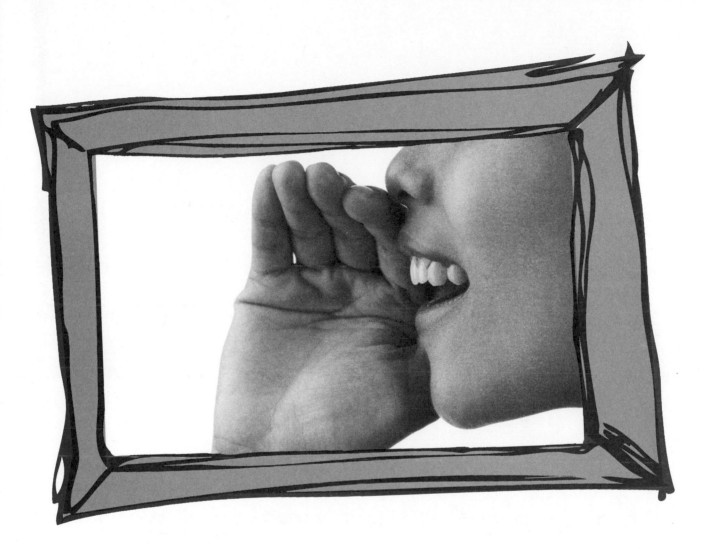

I died in 705. But my **legacy** lives on. I was China's first and only woman ruler.

What would you like to ask me?

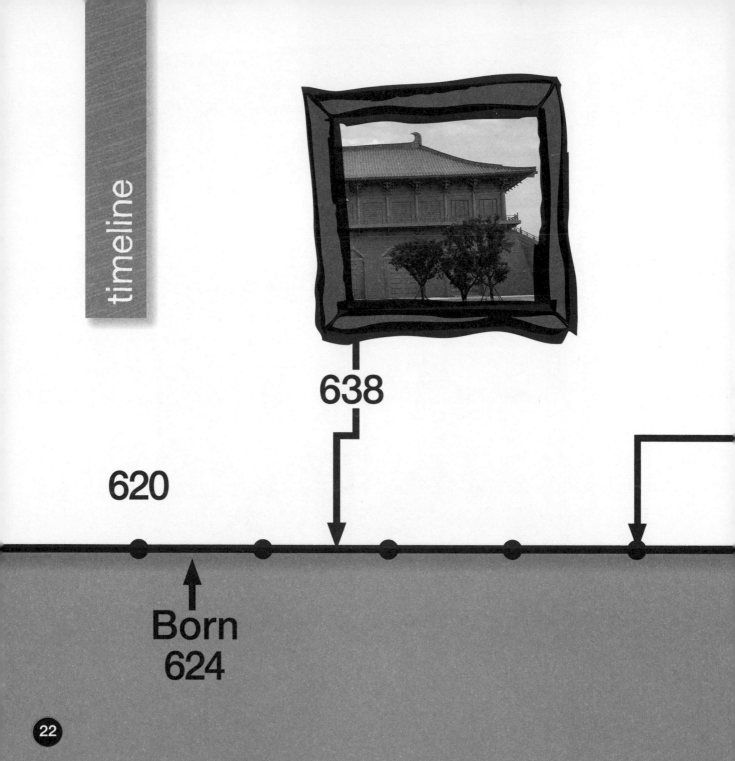

638

620

Born
624

660

720

↑
Died
705

23

glossary

court (KORT) a royal household

emperor (EM-puh-uhr) the male ruler of an empire

empire (EM-pier) a group of nations ruled by one ruler or government

expanded (ik-SPAN-duhd) grew

legacy (LEH-guh-see) anything passed down from a person in the past

rumors (ROO-muhrz) stories that are not proven to be true

index

birth, 4, 22

China, 4–5, 12–20

death, 20, 23

empires, 14

freedoms, 16

marriage, 12

personality, 8, 10

reading and writing, 8–9, 16–17

rulers, 6, 10, 12–21

timeline, 22–23
trade, 14–15